ECO STORIES

For those who

DARE TO CARE

Written by Ben Hubbard
Illustrated by Berat Pekmezci

W
FRANKLIN WATTS
LONDON • SYDNEY

Franklin Watts
First published in Great Britain in 2020
by The Watts Publishing Group
© The Watts Publishing Group

All rights reserved.

Credits
Artwork: Berat Pekmezci
Design: Lisa Peacock
Editors: Sarah Ridley and Paul Rockett

ISBN 978 1 4451 7124 1

Printed in China

Franklin Watts
An imprint of
Hachette Children's Group
Part of The Watts Publishing Group
Carmelite House
50 Victoria Embankment
London EC4Y 0DZ

An Hachette UK Company
www.hachette.co.uk

www.franklinwatts.co.uk

Contents

Introduction

The first modern environmentalist was perhaps Alexander von Humboldt (1769–1859, shown below). He was a German naturalist and explorer who braved giant spiders, electric eels and blood-sucking insects to trek through the Amazon rainforest, up the Andes mountains and down the mines of Mexico. Here, he witnessed first-hand the environmental damage caused by deforestation and mining. Alexander then made a radical observation. He wrote that all living things on Earth were connected. Nature, he said, was a living tapestry that could be unravelled by the harmful activity of humans. This infuriated people in Europe who believed that nature was created for human use. But Alexander von Humboldt was right.

Over two hundred years later, Alexander von Humboldt would have despaired at today's environment. As he predicted, human activity has upset the delicate balance of nature. The burning of fossil fuels in vehicles and power stations has released dangerous amounts of carbon dioxide (CO_2) into the atmosphere. Trapped in the atmosphere, carbon dioxide is making the temperature on Earth rise by absorbing heat that might otherwise have escaped into outer space. The effects of global warming are destroying natural habitats, melting sea ice, making ocean levels rise and causing extreme weather events. Meanwhile, many forests which soak up toxic carbon dioxide are being cut down. The world has reached a climate change crisis.

It is not all desperate news, however. Today's environmentalists remind us that humans can reduce the effects of climate change. They are on the front line of the fight for the Earth. They draw attention to the harmful practices of governments and companies which cause environmental damage and contribute to global warming. Theirs is an increasingly dangerous job: around four environmental activists are killed every week while going about their work. Meanwhile, some world leaders deny climate change is even happening. Others believe it is acceptable to consume large amounts of energy and pollute the world with waste, such as plastic. But plastic is not only clogging up our land and waterways, it is being eaten by fish that humans then consume. We are now literally eating our own rubbish.

These are some of the scientific facts that have spurred many environmentalists, writers, conservationists, broadcasters and activists into action. This book tells the stories of some of these people. Like Alexander von Humboldt, they are the eco heroes who dared to care and stick their lives and reputations on the line. Their aim is to grasp the fraying fabric of nature and stop the environmental ball unravelling. Hopefully their stories will inspire you to join this fight for the planet too.

Greta Thunberg

BORN: 2003　**BORN IN:** STOCKHOLM, SWEDEN　**ROLE:** CLIMATE ACTIVIST

In 2018, 15-year-old Greta Thunberg decided to take matters into her own hands. During Sweden's hottest summer on record, Greta began skipping school to protest outside the Swedish Parliament. She went on strike for three weeks, demanding that politicians take immediate action against climate change. A photo of her soon went viral on social media. Students around the world started their own school strikes and Greta continued to strike every Friday. As Greta made news headlines, world leaders began to take notice.

Greta first found out about climate change when she was eight and was shocked that it wasn't headline news every day. Science showed climate change was destroying the planet, yet no-one seemed to be taking action. This made Greta depressed. At 11, she stopped talking and was diagnosed with Asperger's syndrome, a condition which she says helps her see things more clearly. At home, Greta insists her family are vegan and never take flights.

Today Greta is a household name. She is followed on social media by thousands of teenagers, who stage school strikes against climate change. She is invited to speak at the United Nations, the European Union and the World Economic Forum. Here, she blames the adults in the room for not acting quickly and often repeats the same message: "I want you to act as you would in a crisis. I want you to act as if our house is on fire. Because it is."

Be Inspired!

Greta Thunberg has inspired the world by taking direct action. Her school strikes shame world leaders who have done too little to combat climate change. Greta's message is clear: the world is in a crisis and tomorrow will be too late. It is a scary message but it also delivers hope. This is because it shows young people are willing to take action. You too can join this youth movement. How? By joining a climate change organisation (see pages 46–47), for a start. You can also ask your family to reduce its carbon footprint. Start by reducing energy use, buying less, recycling and cutting down on car travel. The adults have not done enough. Now it is time for young people, like you, to step in.

Chico Mendes

LIVED: 1944–1988   **BORN IN:** XAPURI, BRAZIL   **ROLE:** SOCIAL ACTIVIST

When Chico Mendes turned nine, he began rubber tapping with his father, collecting latex from rubber trees. A rubber tapper makes a cut into a rubber tree's trunk and lets the liquid latex dribble into a cup. It does not damage the tree. But in the mid 1950s, when Chico became a rubber tapper, the Brazilian rubber industry was struggling. Landowners started to cut down rubber trees to make way for cattle farms, making life very hard for rubber tappers and their families.

Chico tried to help by learning to read and write – something not encouraged among rubber tappers. Chico soon found out why. Brazilian rubber tappers were often not being paid properly by their employers. Chico formed a union of rubber tappers with members from all over the capital, Brasília. He was soon protesting about the destruction of the rainforest as well as the rights of rubber tappers. He realised that sustainable forestry practices would stop logging and allow rubber tappers and indigenous people to make a living from the trees. Chico organised human blockades to stop men with chainsaws from cutting down the trees. It worked and brought Chico to the attention of environmentalists worldwide.

By the late 1980s, Chico was a spokesman for the protection of the Amazon rainforest. He brought international attention to the issue. This made the Brazilian government agree to create forest reserves, where local people could use the trees to make a living. Chico's actions, however, had made him many enemies and he was murdered at the age of 44.

Be Inspired!

Chico Mendes showed that people power can create change. He organised rubber tappers into a union and then used non-violent protest to stop the loggers. A group of protesters is a powerful force. Today, protesters often march together for environmental issues. Why not ask your parents if you could go on a march together? You could also form your own group to promote an environmental cause. Ask your teacher if the group can talk to the class. Spreading your message is key. Making people aware of an issue is one step closer to creating change.

Isatou Ceesay

BORN: 1972   **BORN IN:** NJAU, GAMBIA   **ROLE:** RECYCLING QUEEN

As a girl, Isatou Ceesay used fabric bags to carry goods from her village to the local market. But then she discovered plastic bags. These were strong, light and could be thrown away when torn. Plastic bags soon became popular in Isatou's village and across Gambia. However, ripped plastic bags ended up being burned or dumped. When the bags got wet they attracted mosquitoes and disease. Sometimes animals, such as goats, ate the bags and died.

One day, Isatou found a way of cutting used plastic bags into one long strip. She then wove several strips together to make purses, wallets, reusable bags and balls. With a few other women, Isatou set up the Njau Recycling and Income Generating Group in 1998, making money by selling items made from recycled plastic bags. At that time, Gambian women were expected to cook, clean and raise children. Now, these women were able to make a little money for their families by weaving plastic bags as well.

In 2014, the group was renamed Women Initiative the Gambia (WiG). It now has over 2,000 members in 40 Gambian communities. The organisation's work has led to the government banning the import of plastic bags into Gambia. Gambian shops now have to use paper bags or ask people to bring their own reusable bag. Isatou's work has led to a great reduction in plastic waste while also giving many women the chance to learn skills, learn about recycling and bring their families out of poverty.

Be Inspired!

Isatou Ceesay is known as 'the Recycling Queen' because she took a dangerous waste product – plastic – and turned it into something useful that no longer pollutes the environment. Today, most people know the importance of recycling but some people take it a step further by turning their recycling into something new. You could also do this. What could you make from old plastic bottles, for example? You could cut a hole in them and grow plants, make a lamp, or even a boat! Turn to page 46 for more 'upcycling' ideas.

Shōzō Tanaka

LIVED: 1841–1913   **BORN IN:** TOCHIGI, JAPAN   **ROLE:** CONSERVATIONIST PIONEER

Shōzō Tanaka is widely considered to be Japan's first conservationist. He was born in 1841, the son of a village chief, a position he took on at the age of 17. In this job, he tried to bring in reforms and later founded a newspaper focusing on human rights and the relationship between humans and nature. At this time, people were starting to build more factories to make goods. Some of these needed copper, and before long, pollution from the local Ashio Copper Mine began to poison the rivers.

In 1896, disaster struck when the Watarase river flooded. Water polluted with arsenic, mercury and chlorine from the copper mine killed crops in the local rice fields and caused skin sores on people's legs. In addition, toxic smoke from the mine started killing off trees. With no trees to hold soil together, more polluting floods occurred. Local villagers planned a protest against the mine but were stopped by troops.

Shōzō Tanaka kept a careful record of all the pollution caused by the copper mine. Then he took a big risk. He tried to hand a letter about the pollution to Emperor Meiji. Approaching the emperor was forbidden and the guards stopped Shōzō. However, the event created great publicity and Shōzō's letter was published in newspapers. This led to the Factory Law, Japan's first law to prevent industrial pollution. It was a great victory for Shōzō, who spent the rest of his life protesting about environmental issues. He died, penniless, in 1913, after spending all his money on conservation causes.

Be Inspired!

Shōzō Tanaka brought about change through the written word. To prove the Ashio Copper Mine was poisoning the local environment, Shōzō kept a record of exactly what happened. Writers are important in the fight for environmental issues but so is evidence. Some people dismiss environmental issues such as climate change as 'fake news' but factual evidence can show that they are the ones being 'fake'. If there is an environmental issue you are interested in, why not write about it? You could ask your teacher or parent to help you submit your article online. Make sure you have the facts right or you could be accused of spreading fake news.

Dr Helen Caldicott

BORN: 1938 **BORN IN:** MELBOURNE, AUSTRALIA **ROLE:** ANTI-NUCLEAR ACTIVIST

When she was young, Dr Helen Mary Caldicott read a book that scared her. In Nevil Shute's novel *On the Beach*, radioactive fallout from a nuclear war strikes Melbourne in Australia. Born in Melbourne herself, Helen had just graduated as a doctor and understood the devastating effects of radiation on the human body. She decided to pursue two things in her life: medicine and campaigning against nuclear power.

Many people protested against nuclear weapons in the 1970s and 1980s. This was a period of history known as the Cold War, when the United States and the Soviet Union were locked in a nuclear arms race. Global nuclear war seemed a terrible possibility. But Helen added a new voice to those trying to prevent a nuclear apocalypse. As a doctor, she was able to explain the horrifying effects of radiation on the human body. Many people began to take notice. Before long, Helen had become a big name in the anti-nuclear movement. She began touring the world giving lectures about the dangers of nuclear war and nuclear power.

Helen has continued speaking out for over fifty years. As the founding president of the Physicians for Social Responsibility, Helen has recruited tens of thousands of doctors to educate others about the medical dangers of nuclear war and nuclear power. She has also written books and papers about the subject, won countless awards and has 21 honorary degrees. Despite being in her eighties, Helen continues to lecture around the world.

Be Inspired!

Dr Helen Caldicott was inspired by a novel about a particular subject – nuclear war. She then decided to make educating people about nuclear war and nuclear power her life's work. Her knowledge of the terrible effects of radiation poisoning made people take her seriously. In today's world there are many troubling environmental issues. Sometimes it can seem overwhelming so it can be helpful to focus on just one thing. Is there one environmental issue in particular that concerns you? It might be stopping plastic pollution, or planting more trees. Why not concentrate on one issue or cause and become an expert, like Helen? Once you start reading about it, you'll be hooked. Then you can help educate others.

Pablo Fajardo & Luis Yanza

BORN: 1972 (PABLO) AND 1962 (LUIS)   **BORN IN:** ECUADOR
ROLE: LAWYER (PABLO) AND HUMAN-RIGHTS ACTIVIST (LUIS)

As a teenager, Pablo Fajardo witnessed the poor treatment of workers and the Amazon rainforest by oil companies. When he was 18, he was sacked by an oil company for sticking up for his fellow workers. He decided to become a human rights lawyer. In 1993 Pablo met Luis Yanza, an environmental activist representing the indigenous people of Ecuador. The two decided to take legal action against the oil company, Texaco (now called Chevron), for polluting the Amazon in Ecuador.

According to Pablo and Luis, Chevron had spilled millions of litres of crude oil and dumped billions of litres of toxic wastewater into the Amazon rainforest between 1964 and 1990. The pair say this caused an environmental disaster that left the water and land permanently contaminated. This, in turn, led to health problems for local people. Pablo and Luis demanded that Chevron compensate those affected and carry out a clean-up operation in its abandoned drill site.

Pablo and Luis's case against Chevron dragged on for many years. Chevron admitted it had contaminated the water and land but denied this had affected the indigenous people. Pablo and Luis' efforts paid off. In 2012 the court ordered Chevron to pay USD$18.2 billion to 30,000 indigenous people affected by the drilling contamination. However, in a bitter blow, in 2018 an international court ruled that Chevron had cleaned up the area sufficiently and did not have to pay the compensation.

Be Inspired!

The fossil fuels, coal, oil and gas, represent the greatest threat to the environment. The damage occurs when the fossil fuels are extracted and also when they are burned as an energy source, releasing carbon dioxide, one of the causes of global warming. But companies and governments make money from fossil fuels so they resist change. Like Pablo and Luis, you can join a group that puts pressure on companies and governments that support fossil fuel use (see pages 46–47). You can also try to limit your family's use of fossil fuels. By taking small steps, each of us can help protect the global environment.

Dr Jane Goodall

BORN: 1934   **BORN IN:** LONDON, ENGLAND   **ROLE:** SCIENTIST AND ENVIRONMENTALIST

Jane Goodall was always destined to dedicate her life to animal conservation. When she was a toddler, her father bought her a stuffed toy chimpanzee. Family friends thought that the toy would scare her but she took it with her everywhere. She dreamed of going to Africa to see real chimpanzees. When Jane was 23, she was invited to a friend's farm in Kenya. She saved all of her money and sailed to Africa in 1957.

In Kenya, Jane met famous anthropologist Louis Leakey. Leakey offered her the chance of a lifetime: to study chimpanzees. Jane would spend the rest of her life doing this. While living among chimpanzees in Tanzania, Jane made some startling discoveries. She found out that chimpanzees hunted for meat and used sticks as tools to collect termites. Before then people believed that humans were the only animals to use tools. Jane also noticed that chimpanzees showed different emotions and were affectionate like humans, often patting or cuddling each other for comfort.

In 1986, Jane was shocked to learn about the harmful effects of deforestation on the lives of African chimpanzees. She set up the Jane Goodall Institute, a charity focused on wildlife conservation. One of its projects is the Roots & Shoots education programme that teaches young people in over a hundred countries about environmentalism. Today, Jane gives lectures on conservation at conferences around the world. Although she is in her eighties, Jane spends around three hundred days a year travelling to speak to people about this important issue.

Be Inspired!

Jane Goodall's passion is for chimpanzees. For over forty years her main aim was to observe these animals and tell the world about them. But when Jane learned about the harm being done to chimpanzee habitats, her work shifted to trying to conserve animal habitats and the wider environment. Although Jane is only one person, her work has made a great contribution. Jane believes that each person in the world has the personal power to make a difference. She has some great suggestions for how you can make a difference on her Roots & Shoots website (see pages 46–47). By taking small steps, each of us can help reduce our carbon footprint.

Von Hernandez

BORN: 1967 **BORN IN:** QUEZON CITY, PHILIPPINES **ROLE:** ENVIRONMENTAL ACTIVIST

D id you know that every year, millions of tonnes of rubbish are exported from Europe, North America and Australia to Asia? Here, people are paid to recycle the rubbish. However, the rubbish is often contaminated or cannot be recycled so then it is illegally incinerated or dumped in landfill sites or waterways. This harms the local environment and people's health. Von Hernandez decided to take a stand against this environmental damage to his country, the Philippines.

In 1995, Von Hernandez had just joined Greenpeace as Asia Toxics Campaigner, having left his job as an English professor. He became aware of the problems that imported rubbish were causing in the city of Manila. He also discovered that the people of Manila produced around 6,000 tonnes of rubbish a day, most of which was transported to a huge landfill site in his home town of Quezon City. As a solution, the government suggested building giant incinerators to burn the local rubbish, as well as imported rubbish from overseas.

Von led a campaign to stop the government's incinerator plan. The incineration process produces dioxin, a toxic chemical that can poison groundwater and cause birth defects and illnesses. Instead of incineration, Von argued for the rubbish to be recycled and composted. He organised mass protests and a campaign to educate people about the dangers of incineration. It worked: in 1999 the Philippines became the first nation in the world to ban rubbish incineration. Von continues to work for Greenpeace and for Break Free from Plastic.

Be Inspired!

Over 300 million tonnes of plastic are produced every year and recycling it is one of the world's greatest problems. Only around nine per cent of the plastic ever produced has been recycled. The rest has ended up in waterways, seas, landfill sites or incinerators. Despite this, plastic production is predicted to rise by 40 per cent over the next ten years. So what can you do to help? The simple answer is to use less plastic. You can also write to companies to tell them you will not buy their products unless they change to recyclable packaging. There are many environmental organisations you can read about and join on pages 46–47.

Saalumarada Thimmakka

BORN: 1912   **BORN IN:** KARNATAKA, INDIA   **ROLE:** TREE PLANTER AND ENVIRONMENTALIST

Living to over the age of a hundred, Saalumarada Thimmakka is one of India's best known environmental crusaders. Saalumarada's story is a simple one. She used to work as a labourer in a quarry and married one of her co-workers. But after years of marriage, they realised they could not have children. This made Saalumarada very sad. To make herself feel better she began planting trees with her husband along a 4-km stretch of road near her home in the state of Karnataka, India.

Saalumarada began by buying young banyan trees and planting them along the road. After working in the quarry, Saalumarada and her husband carried buckets of water to water the young trees. She grew thorn bushes around them to protect them from being eaten by cattle. Saalumarada took care of the trees as if they were her own children. Over her lifetime, she has been responsible for planting more than eight thousand trees in Karnataka.

For her tree-planting efforts, Saalumarada has won numerous awards and was named one of the world's most influential and inspirational women by the BBC. She is often invited to speak at ceremonies to plant new forests in India and takes up other causes as well, such as campaigning to build a hospital in memory of her husband, who died in 1991. Recently, the Indian government agreed to continue to care for Saalumarada's trees on her behalf.

Be Inspired!

Saalumarada Thimmakka's story is inspiring because it involved such a simple action. Planting trees is something everyone can do and it has also never been so important. Global warming brought about by climate change is in part caused by the destruction of forests around the world. Catastrophic events caused by climate change, such as forest fires, make the problem worse. But planting trees can help reverse this. In July 2019, scientists reported that the planting of one trillion trees could soak up almost two-thirds of the carbon dioxide clogging up Earth's atmosphere. So why not help by planting some trees and encouraging others to do so. Saalumarada planted over eight thousand trees – how many could you plant in your lifetime?

Jacques-Yves Cousteau

LIVED: 1910–1997   **BORN IN:** SAINT-ANDRÉ-DE-CUBZAC, FRANCE
ROLE: EXPLORER, CONSERVATIONIST AND FILMMAKER

Jacques-Yves Cousteau was a French filmmaker who brought the wonders of the oceans to television audiences everywhere. In his early work, however, he was far from the caring conservationist he became later on. In his 1956 documentary, *The Silent World*, the ship accidentally rammed a baby sperm whale; Jacques shot the whale rather than try to save it and his crew massacred sharks feeding on the whale carcass. When he re-released the documentary twenty years later, Jacques refused to edit out these scenes. He said: "It was true and it shows how far we've come and how dreadful humans can be if we don't curtail ourselves."

Jacques made many important contributions to preserving wildlife and the oceans. In the 1960s, he organised a campaign to stop the French government dumping nuclear waste into the Mediterranean Sea. The trains carrying the waste had to turn back when women and children blockaded their way. In 1974, Jacques formed the Cousteau Society, dedicated to marine conservation. In the 1980s, Jacques personally talked to world leaders to try to restrict commercial whaling.

Jacques was also an inventor. He helped develop the diving equipment that allowed his film crew to film underwater and built undersea laboratories where 'oceanauts' could live for days at a time. Jacques made over one hundred and twenty documentaries and wrote fifty books. More and more, these works showed the terrible environmental consequences of human activity in the oceans. Jacques died in 1997, one of the most important marine conservationists of his time.

Be Inspired!

Jacques-Yves Cousteau was a great showman as well as a conservationist. Dressed in his trademark red beanie hat, Jacques brought television audiences face-to-face with the beauty of the ocean environment and the threats it faced through pollution. Documentaries are a good way to reach large audiences and they have never been so easy to make. Today, we can make a film on a mobile phone and broadcast it on websites like YouTube. Why not give this a try? Maybe there is an environmental issue in your local area that you could make a documentary about. Make sure you are entertaining, like Jacques-Yves Cousteau.

Julia Hill

BORN: 1974 **BORN IN:** MISSOURI, USA **ROLE:** ENVIRONMENTAL ACTIVIST

Julia 'Butterfly' Hill became an environmentalist after nearly dying in a car accident. When she had recovered, Julia decided to dedicate her life to making a difference. She joined protesters who were climbing redwood trees in California, USA, to stop them being cut down. Julia volunteered to spend one week in a 1,000-year-old redwood she called Luna. She climbed Luna in December, 1997, and she did not climb down to the ground again for over two years.

Julia said she would not come down until the logging company, Pacific Lumber, promised to stop cutting down redwood trees. She lived on a wooden platform 55 m up and used ropes to pull up supplies from her support team on the ground. She cooked on a small stove and stayed fit by exercising on Luna's branches. In the first year, she faced California's coldest winter on record, living through storms, severe cold and drenching rain. To stay warm, she wrapped herself in her sleeping bag, leaving a small breathing hole.

Pacific Lumber did everything it could to get Julia down. They shone spotlights at her and flew helicopters overhead to scare her. But nothing moved Julia. After 738 days, the company agreed to stop cutting down redwood trees in the area. Julia climbed down and found she was famous. She used her fame to spread the word about protecting forests and today continues her environmental work as an activist for change. Her Circle of Life Foundation aims to change the way humans interact with nature.

Be Inspired!

Julia Hill used a form of non-violent protest called civil disobedience to bring attention to the logging of redwood trees. Civil disobedience means deliberately disobeying rules or laws which are believed unjust. The effect of Julia's protest was to stop the logging. There are all sorts of ways to bring attention to an environmental issue. Is there an issue that you feel strongly about? Why not tell people about it? You could do this through a petition at school or by posting leaflets through people's letterboxes. You could also ask to speak to your local MP (Member of Parliament) about the issue and invite your local newspaper to take photos. As Julia showed, making people aware of an issue can bring great results.

Ken Saro-Wiwa

LIVED: 1941–1995   **BORN IN:** OGONILAND, NIGERIA   **ROLE:** WRITER AND ACTIVIST

Ken Saro-Wiwa was a well-known writer of novels, children's books and television shows before he became an activist. He was born in the village of Bori, Ogoniland, a region of Nigeria where Royal Dutch Shell drilled for oil between 1958 and 1993. Shell extracted oil worth over USD$30 billion but polluted the land in the process. Huge oil puddles replaced farmland, while fish and local wildlife were almost wiped out. Over 550,000 farmers and fishermen were victims of this devastation.

To fight back, Ken co-founded the Movement for the Survival of the Ogoni People (MOSOP). In 1993, MOSOP marched peacefully to demand a share of Shell's Ogoniland profits and compensation for the damage it had caused. But there was a brutal backlash by the Nigerian government. Ken was arrested in connection with the murder of four Ogoni leaders. Meanwhile, the Nigerian army launched a crackdown in Ogoniland, murdering, raping and torturing people.

In 1995, a military court found Ken guilty of murder. Governments around the world condemned this verdict. Shell were asked to intervene in the verdict, but the company did nothing. Ken and eight other activists were hanged. Although Shell has never addressed the pollution it caused in Ogoniland, it was sued for human rights violations: in 2009, Shell paid USD$15.5 million to the families of the men executed by the government. In 2018, the Nigerian government announced it would give USD$1 billion to clean up Ogoniland.

Be Inspired!

The execution of Ken Saro-Wiwa brought condemnation from around the world. Today, he is remembered in books, films and songs. However, Ken's execution is only one example of human rights abuses taking place around the world. About four environmental activists are killed every week for standing up against big business and corrupt politicians that are destroying the environment. So what can you do to help? One way is to join an organisation such as Amnesty International (see page 47). Amnesty and other human rights groups fight to free activists who have been unlawfully imprisoned, as well as bring their stories to the world.

Brianna Fruean

BORN: 1998   **BORN IN:** AUCKLAND, NEW ZEALAND   **ROLE:** CLIMATE CHANGE ACTIVIST

Brianna Fruean is a New Zealand-born Samoan who grew up on her grandfather's stories about life in Samoa, where people have a close connection to the Pacific Ocean. But even during her short lifetime, Brianna noticed changes. The underwater colours were less vibrant and the sea life was harder to find. Brianna realised these were the damaging effects of climate change, alongside increasing numbers of storms, floods and droughts, as well as rising sea levels.

At the age of 11, Brianna began her fight against climate change. She helped found 350.Samoa, an organisation which runs programmes to educate communities and young people in Samoa and other Pacific islands. Brianna says that targeting young people is the best way to bring about change. "It's great to see young people being passionate and not backing down to older people ... all my friends know about Greta Thunberg who has stayed strong and hasn't backed down."

For her work, Brianna has become world famous. At 14, Brianna became the youngest person to attend the United Nations Conference on Sustainable Development; and at 16, she became the youngest person to win the Commonwealth Youth Award. In 2019, Global Citizen named Brianna one of the top 12 female climate activists fighting to save the planet. Today, she continues to speak about climate change and the youth perspective at schools and environmental summits.

Be Inspired!

Brianna Fruean is inspiring because she is not letting her age stop her from being heard. She is one of many young people speaking out about climate change and human rights. This is important – young people are tomorrow's leaders and the damage being done to the Earth today is something they will have to try to fix tomorrow. You are also one of these young people and your voice is as important as anyone else's. You are never too young to get involved. A simple first step is to join a group tackling an environmental issue you feel strongly about. Some of these groups are listed on pages 46–47. Once you are a member, you can think about what your role could be and how to support the cause. It also feels great to be involved in helping the planet.

Gaylord Nelson

LIVED: 1916–2005   **BORN IN:** WISCONSIN, USA   **ROLE:** EARTH DAY FOUNDER

Even as a boy, Gaylord Nelson was an environmentalist. At the age of 14, he organised a tree-planting campaign around his home town in Wisconsin, USA. As an adult, Gaylord would devote his life to protecting the environment. He did this by becoming a politician, first as Governor of Wisconsin and later as a US senator. He would use these positions of power to protect vast areas of land in the USA and draw people's attention to environmental issues.

One of Gaylord's early successes was to use taxes collected from the sale of cigarettes to buy land in Wisconsin and turn it into conservation areas. He then made new laws to stop cleaning liquids being poured into local rivers. This led to Gaylord's environmental agenda, a series of actions that aimed to cut pollution, preserve the natural world and give every American "the right to a decent environment". Part of this agenda was to educate the public about ecology during an annual festival called Earth Day.

The first Earth Day was held in 1970 and attracted over twenty million people in schools, universities and communities across the United States. These people marched in peaceful demonstrations for environmental reform, which led to new environmental laws being passed in 42 US states. Gaylord died in 2005 but Earth Day continues to be celebrated every year by over one billion people across 192 countries. Today, marches, meetings and laws to protect the environment are all planned around Earth Day.

Be Inspired!

Gaylord Nelson was a committed environmentalist who spent his life trying to protect the natural world. His greatest achievement is Earth Day. Events like Earth Day bring together people who all care about the same thing. If you like the sound of this, why not organise an environmental event of your own? It could be to draw attention to a single issue, such as telling people to reuse their shopping bags. First, find some friends who feel the same way as you and have a meeting. Then work out how to tell others (social media, for example) about what you're doing. Finally, organise an event to celebrate your cause. Ask your parents and teachers for help.

Berta Cáceres

LIVED: 1971–2016   **BORN IN:** LA ESPERANZA, HONDURAS   **ROLE:** ENVIRONMENTAL ACTIVIST

I n 2006, construction began on a new dam along the Gualcarque river in Honduras. The Agua Zarca hydro-electric dam was being paid for by foreign investors and was being built by a Chinese firm. However, the dam would cut off the water and food supply for the indigenous Lenca people in the area. It would also stop them from living off the land and the river, which are sacred to the Lenca. Worse still, no one had talked to the Lenca before the dam building began.

One of the local Lenca women was Berta Cáceres, co-founder of the National Council of Popular and Indigenous Organisations of Honduras (COPINH). The group fights for indigenous people affected by logging and building works. When Berta heard about the dam project, she complained to the government. When this had no effect, Berta organised human blockades across the roads to the construction site. The blockades continued for over a year.

Berta's blockades were peaceful but they had to withstand violent attacks by soldiers brought in to remove them. In 2013, troops opened fire, killing one protester and two more the following year. But in 2014, everything changed. The foreign investors and Chinese building firm pulled out of the project and construction came to a halt. But repercussions would follow. In 2016, Berta was shot dead at home. Two years later, four contract killers were convicted of her murder.

Be Inspired!

Berta Cáceres was inspiring because she stood up for people who would otherwise not have a voice. The Agua Zarca Dam would have destroyed the environment and the lives of the local Lenca, but the government and investors did everything they could to build it anyway. Although faced with violence and intimidation, Berta reminded the protesters: "They are afraid of us because we are not afraid of them." In 2019, a pink boat named after Berta was used to block a London road during a climate change protest. It was a fitting tribute. Paying tribute is a great way to remember inspiring environmentalists. If you have felt moved by Berta's story, why not tell others about it? You could write about her for a school project, or speak about her to your class. This way, the brave lives of activists who died for their cause will not be forgotten.

David Suzuki

BORN: 1936   **BORN IN:** VANCOUVER, CANADA   **ROLE:** SCIENCE BROADCASTER

David Suzuki is a long-time environmentalist who says climate change must become the world's first priority. "We're in a giant car heading towards a brick wall and everyone's arguing over where they're going to sit," he says of government inaction to bring about change. David's message is not new – he has been repeating it for many decades as Canada's best loved broadcaster on science, nature and the environment.

David was born just before the outbreak of the Second World War. As the son of Japanese Canadians, he spent several years in an internment camp after Japan declared war on the United States in 1941. David's family then settled in Ontario and he became fascinated by nature, spending his time collecting wildlife from a nearby swamp. As an adult, David studied for university degrees in biology, genetics and zoology and became a professor at the University of British Columbia. But David's real calling was explaining scientific ideas to the public on television. From 1971, he became a regular face on Canadian television, appearing in programmes such as *Suzuki on Science* and *The Nature of Things with David Suzuki*.

David began speaking out against climate change in the 1990s. He created the David Suzuki Foundation to provide research about the environment to the government. He has won multiple awards and is a highly sought-after public speaker. However, he limits his speaking appearances so that he does not increase his carbon footprint through car and air travel. This is because David believes that every person is responsible for doing their part in the fight to save the planet.

Be Inspired!

David Suzuki is an inspiring person because he practises what he preaches. He is a famous celebrity and is paid well when he gives lectures, yet he limits his appearances to a few a year. He has even stopped taking foreign holidays to further reduce his carbon footprint. What is the size of your carbon footprint and how can you reduce it? You can measure your carbon footprint using the websites on page 47. To reduce your carbon footprint, start by making small changes such as: turning off the tap while you brush your teeth and unplugging your electric devices when not in use. Be like David and start your fight against climate change at home.

Dr Wangarĩ Maathai

LIVED: 1940–2011   **BORN IN:** NYERI, KENYA   **ROLE:** GREEN BELT MOVEMENT FOUNDER

Dr Wangarĩ Maathai was born in a village in Kenya and understood the importance of nature from a young age. Her family wanted a good education for Wangarĩ, something that was unusual among village girls at that time. She excelled at school and went on to study for university degrees in the USA and Kenya. When she returned to Kenya to live and work, she realised that poverty was connected to deforestation and the damage this did to the land. She decided to get Kenyans planting trees.

In 1976, Wangarĩ started a community-based tree-planting project which developed into the Green Belt Movement (GBM). The GBM's aim was to reduce poverty and improve the environment by paying village women for every tree they planted. The programme was a huge success and by the beginning of the 21st century, over thirty million trees had been planted. Wangarĩ and other leaders of the GBM began giving lectures across Africa about environmental improvements.

As a result, the GBM's tree-planting programme spread to Tanzania, Ethiopia and Zimbabwe.

Wangarĩ was not only an environmental spokesperson: she was also a supporter of equal rights for women, a cause she often spoke about at meetings of the United Nations General Assembly. She also became a politician, an author and, in 2004, won the Nobel Prize for her environmental and human rights work. Wangarĩ died in 2011 at 71 years old.

Be Inspired!

In 2012, the Wangarĩ Gardens opened in Washington DC, USA, as a memorial to Wangarĩ Maathai. She was an inspiring figure: she flew the flag for environmental change and women's rights. She showed that women can achieve the same positions of power and leadership as men. At a simpler level, Wangarĩ knew the importance of protecting nature. The Wangarĩ Gardens honoured her tree-planting programmes in the best possible way – by planting more trees. You too could plant a garden in honour of Wangarĩ or someone else who has done environmental work. Perhaps there is a bare patch of ground at your school that would work for this. If so, talk to your teachers about buying some trees and design a sign to explain why the garden is there.

Rachel Carson

LIVED: 1907–1964   **BORN IN:** PENNSYLVANIA, USA   **ROLE:** SCIENTIST, CONSERVATIONIST AND WRITER

Rachel Carson was a small, skinny girl who loved nature and reading books. By the age of ten, she was writing for children's magazines and as a teenager decided to study zoology at university. The sea became Rachel's passion and she worked as a marine biologist while writing her first book, *Under the Sea*. She wrote several best-selling books about the sea, which won many awards and made her famous. But Rachel's environmental work would not end with books about the sea.

In 1957, Rachel moved to Maryland, USA, where she became concerned about the spraying of pesticides by the government. Designed to kill fire ants and other insects damaging to crops, the pesticides were also harming the natural environment. Rachel's next and most famous book *Silent Spring* argued against the use of pesticides. It contained secret scientific evidence which linked pesticide use to the destruction of ecosystems and diseases, such as cancer, in humans.

Pesticide companies were extremely critical of *Silent Spring*. However the book won many awards and is credited with inspiring the environmental movement in the USA. It also led to a ban of some pesticides and the formation of the US Environmental Protection Agency. Rachel died in 1964 before the true results of her work became clear but her books continue to inspire people today. She was awarded the Presidential Medal of Freedom by President Jimmy Carter in 1980.

Be Inspired!

Rachel Carson's main weapon in the fight for the environment was her pen. By writing interesting books about the natural world, she made environmentalists out of millions of readers. Her book *Silent Spring* also made it clear that Earth was reaching the limits of what it could take from human activity. For this, many companies tried to discredit her. Now, nearly sixty years later, the environment is at crisis point. More than ever, the world needs writers to explain to the public what is happening in ways they can understand. Why not give it a try? You could write an article about an environmental issue you feel strongly about. Make it interesting, back it up with facts and then try and get it published. You could be the new Rachel Carson for the modern age.

Sir David Attenborough

BORN: 1926   **BORN IN:** LONDON, ENGLAND   **ROLE:** NATURALIST AND BROADCASTER

Sir David Attenborough said recently that he didn't start making wildlife programmes with conservation in mind. Instead, he simply liked observing the natural world. As time passed, David realised that the wildlife he was filming was under threat from climate change. That is when he started to speak out about the need to save the planet.

David started his career in television broadcasting in 1952, although he had only seen one TV programme at that time. He quickly became famous for his programmes that brought the wonders of the natural world directly into people's living rooms. His series *Zoo Quest*, which showed experts collecting wild animals for London Zoo, was very popular with audiences. He went on to make award-winning series such as *Life on Earth*, *The Blue Planet* and *Our Planet*. In his 2019 documentary, *Climate Change – The Facts*, David warned that a failure to tackle global warming could lead to irreversible damage to the natural world as well as the collapse of our societies.

Today, David is often called a 'national treasure', although it is a name he dislikes. He has won countless awards for his documentaries filmed in some of the remotest places on Earth. As well as uniting audiences in admiration, David has always been quick to remind people of the shared human experience: "It is not the differences between us that are important – it is the similarities that are important." Now he hopes that people's love of the natural world will lead to urgent action to preserve it.

Be Inspired!

Sir David Attenborough is one of the most popular TV figures in the world. The support for the environment from such a senior figure is important in spreading the word about climate change. David is most famous as a documentary maker who stopped at nothing to bring TV audiences programmes about the natural world. Why not have a go at making one yourself? All you need is a mobile phone and a good idea. Documentaries can be short, simple and show something from everyday life, such as a snail in your garden. Show your film to friends and family. You could be the next great wildlife documentary maker!

Melati & Isabel Wijsen

BORN: 2000 (MELATI) AND 2002 (ISABEL)   **BORN IN:** BALI, INDONESIA
ROLES: PLASTIC BAG ACTIVISTS

B ali is an Indonesian island famous for its white sandy beaches and sparkling blue waters but it is also gaining a reputation as the plastics rubbish dump of the Pacific Ocean. For local sisters Melati and Isabel Wijsen, whose family home is metres from the beach, the plastic cannot be ignored. When they swim in the sea, plastic bottles bob up around them and plastic bags wrap around their arms. The young sisters decided that something had to change – and quickly.

To tackle the plastic pollution, Melati and Isabel, then only 12 and 10, founded an organisation called Bye Bye Plastic Bags. Its aim is to ban the use of plastic bags on Bali, organise beach clean-up days and create educational material for primary schools in Indonesia. But the sisters decided to go a step further. Inspired by civil disobedience leaders, such as Mahatma Gandhi, they went on hunger strike – and only 24 hours after hearing of the strike, the local governor invited the sisters for a meeting. He promised to support a ban on plastic bags by 2018.

Today, Melati and Isabel meet many politicians and world leaders to promote their cause. They have found promises are quickly made but seldom kept. However, they have had successes. In 2019, a law banning single-use plastic bags on Bali came into effect. The Indonesian government has also committed to reducing plastic pollution by 70 per cent by 2025. Named among the world's most influential teenagers by Forbes, *Time* magazine and CNN, the sisters will be watching their government closely to make sure its commitment is carried out.

Be Inspired!

Melati and Isabel Wijsen are inspiring because they practise what they preach. Neither sister has used a plastic bag since they founded Bye Bye Plastic Bags in 2013. If everyone did the same thing, plastic bags would stop being produced. This would not only dramatically cut back on plastic pollution, but also reduce the carbon footprint of factories making the plastic in the first place. Like the sisters, you can also stop using plastic bags. Simply buy a reusable bag made from fabric and ask every member of you family to do the same. Use it over and over again, until it falls apart. It's an easy step to take and it will help change the world.

Further Information

Have the 'Be Inspired' sections in this book encouraged you to help the environment and fight against climate change? The organisations on these pages are a great place to start. Several of them even belong to the people you have read about in this book. Make sure you have an adult with you when you check out their websites online. Have fun!

Climate Change Organisations

It's easy to become a member of a climate change organisation. Have a look at the websites of some popular organisations below. Each organisation explains how you can sign up and become more involved if you want to.

- Fridays for Future (students striking in honour of Greta Thunberg, see pages 6–7): www.fridaysforfuture.org
- Youth Strike 4 Climate: youthclimatemovement.wordpress.com
- Zero Hour: thisiszerohour.org
- 350.Pacific: 350pacific.org/about/

Upcycling Ideas

Most of us use recycling bins to recycle plastic, glass, paper and tin. But there are loads of creative ways to reuse many of these materials ourselves. This is called 'upcycling'. The links below can show you how to make boats, lamps, plant pots and more. Note, you'll need an adult's help with these projects.

- One Green Planet: www.onegreenplanet.org/lifestyle/fun-upcycling-projects-that-are-perfect-to-make-with-kids/
- Mother Nature Network: www.mnn.com/lifestyle/arts-culture/stories/10-creative-ways-upcycle-your-plastic-bottles
- GB Education: gb.education.com/activity/recycled-crafts/
- Bored Panda: www.boredpanda.com/plastic-bottle-recycling-ideas/?utm_source=google&utm_medium=organic&utm_campaign=organic

Environmental Groups

There are lots of environmental groups that offer education, advice and ways to improve the Earth's eco-systems, like planting trees. Check out some of their websites below.

- Roots and Shoots (Jane Goodall's Foundation, see page 19): www.rootsandshoots.org
- Kids for Saving the Earth: kidsforsavingearth.org
- Kids For a Clean Environment: www.kidsface.org
- Ecology: www.ecology.com

Stop Fossil Fuels

There are several organisations dedicated to stopping the mining and burning of fossil fuels. Find out about their work and how to help them at the links below.

- Go Fossil Free: gofossilfree.org
- People and Planet: peopleandplanet.org/fossil-free
- Greenpeace: www.greenpeace.org/usa/if-we-dont-stop-producing-fossil-fuels-we-wont-make-it/
- 350.org: 350.org

Free from Plastics

There are lots of way to free yourself from using the plastic which is clogging up the Earth's ecosystems and leaving a permanent mark. These websites have some ideas.

- #breakfreefromplastic (Von Hernandez's organisation, see page 21) www.breakfreefromplastic.org
- Bye Bye Plastic Bags (the Wijsen sisters' organisation, see page 45): www.byebyeplasticbags.org
- Plastic Free Schools: www.sas.org.uk/plastic-free-schools/
- Friends of the Earth UK: friendsoftheearth.uk/plastics/living-without-plastic

Human Rights Groups

Below are some of the world's leading human rights' groups. Find out about their latest news, campaigns and ways you can help at the links to their websites below.

- Amnesty International: www.amnesty.org.uk/education/human-rights-young-people-schools
- Human Rights Watch: www.hrw.org
- United Nations International Children's Emergency Fund (UNICEF): www.unicef.org
- Global Citizen: www.globalcitizen.org

Measure your Carbon Footprint

Calculate the size of your carbon footprint and find ways to reduce it using the websites below.

- NASA: climatekids.nasa.gov/review/how-to-help/
- WWF: footprint.wwf.org.uk/#/questionnaire
- PBS: meetthegreens.pbskids.org/features/carbon-calculator.html
- Park City Green: www.parkcitygreen.org/Calculators/Kids-Calculator.aspx

Quote References

Greta Thunberg page 7: 'I want you to act as you would in a crisis': by Greta Thunberg, *Guardian* newspaper, 25 January, 2019.
www.theguardian.com/environment/2019/jan/25/our-house-is-on-fire-greta-thunberg16-urges-leaders-to-act-on-climate

Jacques Cousteau page 25: "It was true and it shows how far we've come": as recalled by Cousteau Society colleague Clark Lee Merriam in *National Geographic* magazine, June 11, 2010.
www.nationalgeographic.com/news/2010/6/100611-jacques-cousteau-100th-anniversary-birthday-legacy-google

Brianna Fruean page 31: "It's great to see young people being passionate" by Brianna Fruean et al in the *Guardian* newspaper, 15 March, 2019.
www.theguardian.com/commentisfree/2019/mar/15/young-climate-activists-striking-today-campaigners

David Suzuki page 37: "We're in a giant car heading towards a brick wall" as quoted in the *Toronto Daily News* by Erika Tucker, 13 April, 2012.
globalnews.ca/news/233616/top-10-memorable-david-suzuki-quotes/

Glossary

anthropologist An expert in anthropology, the study of human societies.

Asperger's syndrome A form of autism, which may make sufferers awkward in social situations or preoccupied with a single interest.

carbon dioxide (CO₂) A colourless gas produced by burning carbon.

carbon footprint The amount of greenhouse gas emissions (particularly carbon dioxide) that each person is responsible for through their lifestyle.

carcass The dead body of an animal.

climate change A change in global climate patterns caused by increased carbon dioxide in the atmosphere, which is in turn caused by the burning of fossil fuels.

compensate To give money to a person or group in recognition of loss, suffering, injury or death.

crusader A person who dedicates themselves to bringing about social, political or environmental change.

deforestation The process of clearing a forest by cutting down its trees.

environmentalist A person concerned about protecting the environment and the effects of pollution.

incinerated Destroy something by burning it.

indigenous people The people who have lived in a land from the earliest times.

latex The milky substance found in the rubber tree that can be manufactured into rubber for commercial use.

legislation Laws enacted by a government.

pesticide A toxic spray used to destroy insects or other animals that destroy plants or crops.

radiation Extremely harmful electromagnetic waves caused by a nuclear explosion.

upcycling Reusing a discarded product to make something else that is usable.

Index